ALTERNATE MEANS OF TRANSPORT

Poems by CYNTHIA MACDONALD

ALTERNATE MEANS OF TRANSPORT

*For Virginia, one of
the special Virginias.
Love,
Cynthia*

Alfred A. Knopf   New York   1985

THIS IS A BORZOI BOOK
PUBLISHED BY ALFRED A. KNOPF, INC.

Some of the poems were first published in the following periodicals:
*American Poetry Review, The Iowa Review, Massachusetts Review,
The New Yorker, Poetry Northwest,* and *Shenandoah.*
"Apartments on First Avenue" was first published in *New York: Poems,*
ed. Howard Moss, published by Avon Books in 1980.

Library of Congress Cataloging in Publication Data
Macdonald, Cynthia.
Alternate means of transport.
(Knopf poetry series; no. 19)
I. Title.
PS3563.A276A93 1985   811'.54   84–48739
ISBN 0–394–54386–6
ISBN 0–394–72968–4 (pbk.)

Manufactured in the United States of America
First Edition

For my father, Leonard Lee; his father, Leonard C. Lee; and his grandfather Leonard C. Levy. I have wanted for some time to take back my great-grandfather's name; had I not been cautioned about the confusion caused by authors' name changes, this book would have listed the author as Cynthia Levy-Macdonald. In the invisible writing of families, that is how it reads.

~ The use of this symbol indicates a stanza break at the bottom of the page.

I ALTERNATE MEANS OF TRANSPORT

A SEQUENCE

I THE LAWN: NEW DESIGNS

Hats blow away, sailing, swirling over
The bright green lawn—mostly straws: boaters, panamas,
The pale, large-brimmed ladies' versions, sailors,
Streamers and ribands fluttering like kite tails,
Leghorns of Tuscan wheaten straw, its color clear,
Delicate and golden, crenelated towers of Irish thicket straw,
A few cloches for those who like to wear
Their halos pulled down over their ears.

But also, silk hats, buckram-bodied, patterned with
A plush of brilliant gloss or varnish-stiffened calico,
Wimples, tops, velvet mob caps like heavy breasts, cocked
Of straw and felt, lace milking tams, one Flaundrish beaver.
And the panoply of people chasing, twirling,
Tripping, jumping. Ballet after Bournonville on the green.
Painting after Brueghel, repainted Chagall, on the green.

~

Everyone but the man with a butterfly net is laughing
Or smiling; such amiable pursuits.
Some of the high-flyers are swathed in veils—
Victorian clouds—or spangled mantillas where the sun
Strikes a patch of mist. The commotion, synchronized as
The word tells us, amazing in such a small space,
That verdant lawn on the head of a pin. For of course they,
Like us, are minuscule and lose their heads even more easily.
They will continue their *Hosanna*s and *Salva Me*s
No matter what. No matter . . . or so some say.

The man with the butterfly net, enthralled by quarrels of
Glass but not of words, inspects the action of
A Spangled Fritillary's wings, which might yield a new model
For the community. He envisions the firmament suffused
With orange and black as the Host descends wearing his creation.
A flutter of descent, yes, orange and black, as if snow
Had taken on the colors of All Hallow's Eve,
Leaving the sanctity of white for something less determinate.
The Spangled Fritillary alights on a lilac's flowery fist.
The net fills with air, as if it were a capuchin, and
Rings the branch enveloping its prey.

The Curator lectures on "The Triptych of Heaven and Hell" by
Capelli, "See the border friezes of angels repeating
The lower motifs of clustering stars." He is using
His pointer of light to pick out details of the work;
Circles of light halo this figure or that, giving it
The strange magnification of tight focus.
"See the Jew skating, the man in his nightclothes
Chasing the visibles with his butterfly net, see the organist.
And there I am in the left-hand corner of the center panel;
See the circle of my light ringing the blue and white saucer
From which the cat is licking cream thick as paint.
The painter, too, is there: yes, the man with the net,
But also the prisoner, the acolyte, the lover stroking
The buttocks of his love whose leghorn, trimmed with
Daisies and red ribands, lies beside her on the grass,
The woman carrying a boil pot and a protest banner.
Look further: how many other places can you locate the painter?"
A sudden wind blows through the gallery where they stand
Listening to the lecture. The lighter hats threaten to lift,
Tugging at the hairpins of some of the bystanders,
But the touch of a hand is enough to subdue them.

The bearded Jew skates differently as he practices
His curls, addressing the ice with rabbinical argument.

A certain stiff grace in the arms and thin chest, a wiggle
In the hips as if something out of Salome remains embedded there.

He stands out on ice embroidered by everyone else twirling
(Whirling), gliding (sliding), checking

(Pecking with the beaks of their skates). He knows he is
Distinct from all the others and wonders again, why?

His solemnity? No; the oriental girl repeating eights is equally;
So is the boy practicing hockey moves, goals, the hat trick.

And the whole beginners' class flapping
Across the ice like newborn chicks.

Is it because of what he writes with the blades of his skates,
Determined to keep the words of the Torah alive

By inscribing them on ice? He knows that he has never
Been able to answer, has been forced to accept

A strange combination of fear and pride which he cannot
Lose, cannot outrace, does not wish to outrace.

In mirrors at the side of the rink he sees the halo
His hair makes around his yarmulke and around the hair

~

A circle of white moths like the rings of Jupiter,
Like flakes of light, like the swirl of snow around

An empty bird's nest, and wonders if he forgot
To put camphor in the woolens last spring.

Figure 8: The Chaos of the Elements

The lower waters have now been stirred into a confused and "undigested" mass, in which the four elements fight against each other: hot against cold, wet against dry. Manly P. Hall has pointed out the resemblance of this figure to the human intestines. Fludd himself makes the bowels in man equivalent to the elemental realm in the universe.

Joscelyn Godwin, ROBERT FLUDD

4   THE ROLE OF HATS IN ILLNESS

Here we see the water converted by the fire
Into a vapour, which ascends from the pot and meets
The pot's hat whose lower temperature makes it condense
Into drops. It is even so with the human body:

The watery phlegm originates in the southerly region of
The intestines and in disease is heated by
The fire of the liver; it rises again on the third day
To the colder region of the head where it coalesces in
Warm droplets. These are the cause of ear infection,
Sattin coughs, torn veils, moth holes, catarrh and coryza.
The body's mean has tippled so one suffers side effects of
Headache, aesthetic fault and all forms of bonnet vertigo.

The organist plays the Michaelmas Magnificat,
Each needle of sound a silver spike
Crowning his head. It is his work; as Kappelmeister
He both writes and plays. At his feet, there is
A basin for slops, the debris from the nether region
With its tumescent liver, its coils of lights,
Its laden kidneys, its decomposing spleen.
Delivering music, he picks the basin up and puts it on.
It rests uncomfortably atop the spiked crown, driving
The heavenly deeper into his head as he leaves for bed.

The felts meet in Congress: they cast
Lots, salt, everything to the wind.
And couple.

The peaked caps, engorged with braid, meet
In a dictatorship: they cast
Lots, pillars, statues of the leader, firing
Them in the oven for days.

The straws are the most disorganized: they cast
Lots to see which head they wish to crown
On this glorious summer day
Which is itself impervious
To the body politic.

And when they have put on cloak, rapier, plumed hat, scarlet-gold-tissue breeches, etc., they descend to the women and order feasting to commence. If they follow the wisdom of Avicenna, they will alternate all the windy meats with a decoction of the condite fruit of wild rose, parsley roots and centaury until lust issues forth, breeding all that is copious and universal, those divers truths which divert humors, aches, winds, etc.

Oliver Rowland, REMEDIES AGAINST DISCONTENTS

7 BENEFIT BALL FOR SAVE THE CHILDREN

Great scurfs of food are borne in, piled so high they
Drip onto embroidered carpets where lovers, bare of
Hats, lie entwined. The serving men step over them
Lifting roasts and joints, towering jellies shaking their
Church colors, nests of tatted squab and quail, berries
Staining clotted cream, bisques, broths, chowders, thorny
Silhouettes of artichoke and pineapple, pastries and pasties
Oozing drops of kidney juice and bits of beef, and all
The nouns of nourishment too crammed with
Stuff and sauce to make their source discernible.

There is finally enough so that if food be the food of
Love they can play on and in it and, satiated, be carried off
In great scurfs, as if the scales of extinct animals,
The platters on which they sprawl, were music and
The rocking motion came from the wind, not from
The apprehension that, in an agony of indigestion, they
Have turned their hats into pudding basins, into
Breast adornments, into buttock fetish bowls, denying
The struggle that circular shapes insist on if
They are to serve at all. These lovers see the universe as

Self-contained, a metaphor, they state, which has the ring
Of truth. And they twist and turn on their scurfs
Feeling that inside of them, in an agony of indigestion,
The maw of the universe is farting something which
Could not possibly be hats.

"Here there are flights of angels like
Small albino flies. See the fine-haired robes,
The glassen wings, the compound eyes. They crowd
The field within the frame. Note the multiplicity
Inside those eyes. The seraphim within, reflected by
The pupils of cherubim. You look confused.

"Actually what you are frowning at is white canvas,
Paint still in the vat, a snow field on which we,
Who understand the many shades of meaning, will paint.
The artist has at hand only the hues of his short span,
The transports of his time. But every century
Critics create afresh the apprehending vision."

The wind asserts its will, sweeping the museum,
The negative wind of fire, sucking,
Giving vent, inhaling the curator, the bystanders,
The painting and the wall on which it hangs,
The museum entire in fiery discontent.

Albertus conjectured, and put "each choir at 6,666 legions, and each legion at 6,666 angels." But demons are winged horses of another color. Unlike the angels, these apes of God are capable of reproducing their kind. What is more, as Origen alerts us, "they multiply like flies." So today there must be a truly staggering horde of them. The problem of population explosion here is clearly something to worry about.

Gustav Davidson, A DICTIONARY OF ANGELS

9 THE C MAJOR MASS WITH FLIES

Flies invade the eyes of the people drowsing on
The south lawn. The fly bodies, in their black,
Mother-of-pearl casings, carry eggs to be laid
In the pupil's optic dark. Wings, soldered
Like the leaded glass of Gothic glaziers, fold in
After entry.

Flies in the eyes enact the flying that is in
Each of them, all goggle and sequin virtuosity—
World War I aces—all act and axe—hatchet murderers
On the moor. The liquid drowse of noon is stopped
By the agony of penetration, itch, encrustation
As flies mate and leave the eye's incubator
To circle around heads; halos of flies,
Crowns of flies, shimmering, musical, open to
Interpretation.

The people on the dry, smooth-shaven lawn begin to run,
Circling in steps like those of the generations of
Hat-chasers but they wear no hats, only
Masses of flies in their open buzzing circles;
And the people run to escape reinvasion, smelling

Rank fruit as they wave their arms hoping
To dispel the tarnished silver clouds of vertu
Turned; run and twist, Graham dancers on the green.
And exterminators seed abandoned hats,
Which could be bowls of incubation,
With toxins.

The cycle is beyond human agency;
Flies intent without intention on their performance
Of *Paradise* penetrate deep into the set of
The eye which is painted brighter than
Crimson Lake or Crystal Azure. Flies of
The evening's Mass emerge from the wings,
Work their way forward like ranks of soldiers
Or counter choirs. Even in this time of indecision
Certain agonies induce in the most languid, a need
For solutions: argyrol, silver nitrate, gentian violet.
But . . . not yet. Not yet. Only
A glimmer of hope.

The Jewish Talmudists take upon them to determine how God spends His whole time . . . sometimes overseeing the world, etc., like Lucian's Jupiter, that spent much of the year painting butterflies' wings, and seeing who offered sacrifice; telling the hours when it should rain, how much snow should fall in such a place, which way the wind should stand in Greece, which way in Africa.

Robert Burton, THE ANATOMY OF MELANCHOLY

10   THE GLASS-WALLED CONSERVATORY

The man with the butterfly net has given up on wings.
He sits at the drawing board applying the shape of crystals
To the shape of hats: lace, facet, line of fault.
"More applicable to heads," he says, bending over the board,
Drawing essential structures so finely delineated
They rise off the page like the angels they are meant to adorn.

His name begins with *L* or so the others who call him insist—
Leonardo, Lucifer, Li Po. . . . He answers indifferently,
Knowing that in his century cause and effect are blurred
And everything turns back upon itself. The Sistine Chapel ceiling,
As close to heaven as many feel they will come, is most easily
Looked at for long periods of time by holding
A mirror in your hands and looking down.

In the night sky around the Conservatory, hats
Are going past in flames. Hat meteors, hat fire storms
Flash past as L. continues to draw. The heavenly host
Watches its visible badge of sanctity
Decorate the heavens with fiery hoops and loops as if
A circus arena were being set for tygers. The host
Squints as the halos move further out
And settle over spheres to marry—bright, varnished rings
Around the planets of distant galaxies.

Through the balance of terror, we all come to hold a dagger to the hearts of those nearest and dearest to us as well as to threaten those far away . . . The parent threatens the child, the lover the lover, the friend the friend, the citizen the citizen. Our acceptance of nuclear weapons is in that sense a default of parenthood, of love, of friendship, of citizenship . . . And in making a "conscious choice" to lift the nuclear peril . . . we resolve to clear the air of the smell of burning flesh.
Jonathan Schell, THE ABOLITION

II THE HAT FACTORY

The hat in the hands of the hatmaker catches fire.
She is not surprised; she has always thought one would;
The heat where she works causes inflammation every summer.
Not for nothing did the garment center give birth
To the term sweatshop. Flames lick the brim. Storms
Caused by atmospheric tension break, and the spot
Where the roof has always leaked acts as a fire extinguisher.
"Piss pot," she says, holding the felt in her hands.
Blisters rise on them. The burns are not too bad.
But what about the children alone at home?

With what astonishment he saw the silk dresses with great gauze wings pinned to their backs by scarab brooches catch fire just as the band concert began, as if breath from the sounding brasses fanned the flames. It was a moment when his vision of the redemptive had to be recovered again, as if history were only an old sofa.

Placido Santos, STOREHOUSE OF REMARKABLE ATONEMENTS

12 THERE CAME A WIND

Hats fly around the museum as the wind
Grows from zephyr to breeze reversing
The order of things. In moments of
Abatement when it seems *the ominous is past,*
And the universe has stopped breathing,
Hats come to rest

> On the heads of Nefertiti, Aphrodite,
> The Thinker (3rd casting), the Degas ballerina
> In her gauze tutu, on the discus of
> The Discus Thrower, the spear of the knight
> In the Great Hall of Armor, on the penis of
> One of the putti circling King Oswin's bed,
> On the breast hole of a reclining Henry Moore,
> On the cross being readied for Christ,
> On Cleopatra's needle and on and on.

The bystanders chasing their hats
Begin to laugh at the odd adornments;
Even the curator permits himself a smile.
And the wind runs through the fingers of statues
And slides along the frames of paintings,
Making music out of art. And the hats,

Like mutes of trumpets or trombones,
Damp the sound down just enough
So there is no pain for those in the halls and galleries,
Only a dancing exhilaration. And out through
The mouth and eyes of the Museum music spills down the Avenue.

13 A FLOURISH OF CASUAL KILLING

The glass dome of Heaven above the Conservatory
Falls in from the aftershock, cutting the soft parts
Of the night sky to shreds. Black shreds and glass
Imprinted with galaxies and hat nebulae shower down,
Announcing in a flourish of fragments that
The universe is both finite and infinite.

For those alone and makeless there is the carnal pleasure of
Hats, genital amazements as the *bracelet of bright hair*
About the bone is capped: an ocelot toque, a tam-o'-shanter,
Loose slide of Muslim veil, loll of sateen bagnolette,
Anthem tattoo of helmet pot and all,
All only exquisite mimicry of flesh on flesh, as planetarium
Stars, the sky and cats, the cry of babies.

After beatitude, the lonely rise, not with the calm
Swelling of bread but with marsh fever, malarial
In its reliefs and returns. The lonely call for order,
Invoking clerical devices: fasts, strict columns,
A new and secret prison of the pulses, no more loose ends.

~

Where like a pillow on a bed, a pregnant hat swells up
Its yield will be a relic of desire,
A bronzed bonnet on the bedside table and
The knowledge of those alone: what's done cannot be
Undone; our enmities unite us, not our loves.

14 DEPENDING ON THE SALVATION OF HATS

The people are gone.
Only the hats remain (reminding us
Of man's capacity for destruction).
Visible badges of sanctity litter
The spangled heavens long after
What we value them for is extinct,
Reminding us, tugging
At our hems or trousers
Like a child wanting attention,
That the child's hat may be here
Long after the child,
That half-lives of bliss or torment,
Lies of escape routes are
Equally irrelevant and that if
This is true, it is an obvious lie,
Addressed as it must be,
If true, to hats.
We try to keep the underlying truths
Where we can't see them, that boy
In the story with the rich butter,
Cool stream butter, under
The protection of his hat,
Walking, twirling, jumping
In the radiance of the sun.

The problems resulting from defining and describing complex conflicts by use of simple conflict models are manifold. Almost tautologically, we can say that as a consequence of this simple modelling, the complex conflict will be represented in an oversimplified fashion.

Frank Moulaert, "On the Nature and Scope of Complex Conflicts"

PEACE SCIENCE SOCIETY

15   THE DIALECTIC OF THE HATLESS

The curator is fondling tiger's-eye cufflinks,
The Jew is shopping at the Safeway, the man with the net
Is drawing in the Conservatory, the hatmaker is
Reading *Crusaders in the Bosphorus* to her children,
The organist is lying in the stained sheets of his scurf,
Transported by his new cantata, "The Golden Mean,"
The curator is lecturing the painter, who is filing her nails,
"The trouble is, in a time without absolutes,
God's will, the King's, the family's, the tribe's,
No longer crowned with certainty, one understands
How tedious absolute freedom is."
"No. How frightening. Yet, perhaps a form of bliss.
The liquefaction of our hats may force salvation on us," she says.
"I would like to frame these dilemmas for you," he says.
"You always do. I'm returning to the lawn."

The man with the net is drawing in the Conservatory,
Pulling the strings tighter, making sure that
What can be secure is; the organist is staring at
The bronze hat on his bureau, the Jew
And the hatmaker are drinking tea,
"Isn't it only your own death and, possibly,

The destruction of what you, yourself, have made—
Music, books, flower beds—that you can really feel?"
"Only your children," says the hatmaker, giving suck to
The rosy mouth of her youngest. "Also," says the Jew
Who has no children, "your hats."

I have always found that Angels will have the vanity to speak of them-
selves as the only wise; this they do with a confident insolence sprout-
ing from systematic reasoning.

Blake, "The Marriage of Heaven and Hell"

16 AT THE ROUND EARTH'S ENDURING CORNERS

If we, all brimless, had the comfort of hats,
Or even if we did not but were sure they, with
Their hats, were standing there all pins and needles
To save us, filling the sky with the snow of
Their muslin boaters, their immaculate certainties,
We could relax into that sureness which the cleavage
Of good into good and evil brings. Instead,
We consult language, a paltry vehicle
For salvation. See how it falters,
Deprived of hats and hosannas.
    No . . . Not yet . . .
Is what we are left with. No epiphany or apotheosis.
The net of glittering firmaments
Now pin-pointed as what it is.
    And yet, perhaps . . . Hush don't raise . . .
    Or is . . . Keep it under your . . .
It is unspeakable.
    Perhaps that is why . . . We may live after . . .
    Perhaps . . .
A quiet ending.

Paradox is not comfortable; its X exposes that; too many
Cross-purposes to allow you to settle exquisitely poised
As a Spangled Fritillary on the lace of a blooming lilac branch,
As the sexless angels on the head of a pin.

O A B C D angels says Leonardo.
M R no angels says the Jew, Y Z what can't be?
The bystanders wring their hands as if they were bells.
Stop playing, they tell the organist and the poet,

And both could, could make a surface
Clear, calm and reflective, a voluptuous skin,
Giving lap and lull, lap and lull. I could
Take you back to the lawn, now studded

With its spring brocade of flowers, to a sky
Studded with hats, to a sky lavish with hats.
Poems lavish with the language of light wing through a time when
We are in the dark. Illuminated by static, by the electricity

Of the synthetic, love—a plain song, a plaint—is asked
To do more than it can. It is, perhaps, what we have left.

II   THE TUNE
HE SAW

for Arnold Goldman because he
could not have his favorite

THE TUNE HE SAW

Woods. A stand, waiting for the bite, the teeth.
Joshua Briggs picks logs from the stack he's cut,
Sticks them in the black belly, fixing dinner—
Pork, beans and slaw—before the night's concert.
Tunes shimmy in pieces. He looks out at his lot, his stand of
Woods. Notes the green. That shine.
"Play a tune on a jug; the moon pops out like a cork.
But that's nothing to playing a saw."

He puts in his teeth for the slaw. Sweet sap, molasses,
Spreads around hillocks of salt pork into it.
The Moonlight Sonata hangs over his head.
And the light of the saw. "You can use it to cut, too.
That very same instrument." His parcel of
Woods. Pieces of green; the notation of trunks and
The land, that ground bass over which his
Single strand of tune will soar like an angel.

"Lots of people my age like a tune.
Today it's all beat but I give them music."
He begins to practice. The saw bends.
Quavering moonlight fills the room. The saw
Arches and twists between hand and thigh.
He strokes it with his bow, "A cello bow made
From manes of white Argentine horses. That country's got
Silver in its name." The saw angles and dips
Like a waterfall between hand and thigh.

The semi-, demi-, hemi-quavers, the crotchets of
Wood are joined as Joshua Briggs

Bends what he saw. The tune rises like the holy ghost.
It will rise, that Moonlight Sonata,
Above the audience at the Grange
Like the host. He will greet them with music.
His white forelock falls over his eyes as he bows, twisting
Silver between hand and thigh.
He describes the tune in the air, sawing it into
Parcels of light. "Angels are women; I know that."
The room is full of what he can accept.

WHY PENELOPE WAS HAPPY

Taking the carrots away from the slave who is peeling them,
Penelope slices, seeing
Wild asses in the woods, woods green and tender as spring lettuce,
Woods dappled silver as the talents of men gambling in market sun.
Ulysses is in that wood.
She knows it; seers recognize their visions as distinct from other seeing.
Tears run down her cheeks and
Seep through her rosy fingers onto the carrots.
She hands the splayed bunch back to the slave, saving only one.

To her dawn room, the place where light first pries
Its illumination through the columns, to her loom, one of many woven
Through the palace like the alabaster urns, urns full of
Dark wine to remind them of the sea.
Seated, she replaces her olive wood shuttle with the carrot,
"Show me again where he is." Yellow threads ravel
From it, like hair, to become sun on the forest floor.
Ulysses stands, a boar's bladder
To his lips, wine trickling through his beard,
Streaking its silver threads red.
She weeps with happiness. He is safe and
Far.
"Daphne watch over him," she prays, weaving leaves of laurel.

To be alone in your domain—
A queen within, a king without and distant—
Such stately pleasure, such companied solitude.
Now he and his men are boarding the barque, herding the wild asses
Who bray with fear before them. Now they are setting sail.
Now they are safely at bay.

The barque's cheek paint reflects its unwinking eye in the water's glaze,
Soothing the Gods. Her unpainted cheek flares
As late morning light
Pries its way through the columns
To touch her, a sign
It is time to move to the noon room where she will work on Apollo,
Burning her fingers as she caresses the golden threads of his hair.

DEGREES OF PEN/MAN/SHIP

(from Traveling up the Nile)

First he checks his immaculate whites,
Then the life preservers of his *O*s, the troughs
Of his *W* s, the breasts of his *E* s; direction,
Slant, degree, compass, the evenness of
His disposition. Much depends on his capacity
For perfection: *f* and *f* so much alike yet
Minutely differentiated: a *f*irst and *f*econd,
f uck and *f* ix, *f*ire and *f* ix.

Abandoning sail and adopting steam, he uses
The Palmer method. The coins of his *O* s
Appear, golden, in the air, clink to the deck,
Roll over the brink, cut the surf to the
O O O s of the passengers. *f* s manifest themselves
As cargo, blinking, trying to see what
He has up his sleeve. Deckhands applaud
As brilliant scarves float from his fingers
Spreading silk upon the sea.
The Palmer method no longer makes it
Possible to confuse what is seen with the fee.

As a prize for being first in his class
He receives his Captain's stripe and a pen,
Not goose, that spine with lacquered *V* s
Suited for cuneiform, but ostrich, quill and
Softest curlicues. He takes off
His uniform, writes on, flaring his ready lights,
Writes words on skin, the tickle of ostrich,

The stroke of the quill, rounding the navel,
Moving down toward the canal, the locks,
The waves of Egyptian bliss. No surfeit here.

DEATH ON THE HIGH SEAS

for the baritone Leonard Warren and my father, Leonard Lee

The oil-thick green-and-blue of the breakers catches
The false morning light. Sun, #12 flood-bright,
Astounds the neurons of his eyes
Causing a moment of pain and blindness.

O say can you see by the dawn's early light threads
Through the heavier sound. No. That is Butterfly:
Steam not sail, Japan not the fjords. His ears hurt
As if he were in a plane of thin air. Stage walls are always
Flat but now Senta is, too: transubstantiation, perhaps.
He pushes the curtain of music aside, grasping a clearer
Weave of light, remembering he has not sung Sharpless for years.

Hounded, never allowed land, the Hollander must sail,
A middle-aged mariner who sold his soul for stardom.
His circuits of the seas are as random as
Bargains with the Devil are rigid. He longs for land
But has it only every seven years to search for a woman
Who loves him enough.

Each time he marries. I am the first issue,
A source of continual argument. Fathering is an expected
Part of fortune, a patriotic act, though those who knew
My father agree he was tone deaf: only when they all
Stood up did he recognize the anthem.

At night the sea's blue banner reflects
The star spots in a pox of patriotism and the Dutchman,

Tossing waves of white hair, sings of this barque
To which he is chained. He tries to break out
But the needles of false stars weld with the rods
Of his vision and he is forced by the pain of movement
To remain still. Only his arms gesture as he sings:
Wohl hub auch ich voll Sehnsucht meine Blicke.
Aus tiefer Nacht empor zu einem Weib. As a storm
Blows windward, the leitmotif warns us of what is to come.

The third time love frees him. A spangle of light
Veils her hair as they wed. He has no more children,
Choosing to breed basset hounds instead. To live
He coins phrases. Every night the broad sweep of
Klieg lights celebrates Hollywood's occasions and
His joy. Their love is so deep that even in Southern Cal.
They share a car. But the devil keeps his bargains
Only to the letter. Cancer. And father, alone with
His hounds, finds dogs are not enough to follow
In his footsteps. Still young, he determines this stage
Will be the last; meticulous, he arranges the morning light.

The boat rolls in the waves and floods with regrets,
Formed and ephemeral as foam. The singer,
Recognizing *The Force of Destiny*, knows this will never
Be his role; Senta will die for another.
He tries to pull off his character as if it were
A diving suit; too late; the hemorrhage begins
Center stage. Too late, as well, for father and daughter:
One so stern; one refusing to bow. What they have
Amassed cannot save him. They try to change characters,
To sluice them clear with the flooding water,
But the ink is indelible. They try to pay off

The devil, rolling silver dimes in pages but, wet,
The paper breaks and change escapes for good.

Leonard, Leonard, lions linked by the distance of what was
Lionized and longed for: my baritone, my father,
Neither can lie with the lee. Both the managed and
Unmanaged deaths—the exploding artery, the exploding gun—
Are acts of piracy. Silver coins reflect off the water
As the steersman sights land and anoints death with music,
Running up a black flag on the high C.

THE FOUR VIRGINIAS

for Virginia Carmichael

When Priss is in Virginia, she is very careful not
    To fall apart. Her father, whose grandfather changed his name from
Levy to Lee, taught her that the birthplace of presidents induces
    A state of caution, knowing that family trees can be
Dangerous as standing under one in lightning storms and the bough
    Breaks and the cradle falls and you have to be *so* careful
Of a baby sister. So she is very careful not to fall apart,
    Poking Virginia's mouth to make sure she has no teeth.
Priss *was* careful even though Virginia cried.
    The columns of Virginia's addition were neat as Mount Vernon's
Although she was cross-eyed because she got a weak muscle which was
    Too bad and made it hard to tell she was telling the truth
When Priss lied and bit her arm and said Virginia'd done it.

    Imperfection, as we all know, is looked at askance in
First families especially those with impeccable new names so
    Even when she is not in Virginia she is very careful,
Remembering particularly the dismembered doll and its consequences.
    Her father said the undertaker said Virginia was beautiful
In her coffin though he wouldn't look and had her
    Sealed up. But Virginia is beautiful even when she falls apart
Though Priss disdains her state as if Priss were the DAR denying
    Constitution Hall. Realize, though, Virginia
Is not the first family because she is the father's second wife
    And look! Virginia is falling apart. Pearls of tears form
In the socket cups where her eyes rest like grey oysters.

~

How painful it must be to extrude a pearl. Like a gallstone,
Priss imagines as if she did not know. Pretty Virginia with
    Her round hill breasts and curves and rivers and breathy bays.
Pretty Virginia, so pretty with her calm face like a doll's,
    The head of a doll in a puddle on the roof where
You could look across the street at the Lenox Hill interns lying
    On the beds of the nurses with the nurses and, oh dear,
Virginia is falling and this time Priss cannot look because
    There is something in her eye, a piece of grit or soot
Which must be lacquered over because only Virginia who falls
    Is allowed to though she must have been put back together
Because see, see she is stretching her arms languidly and smiling
    With her perfect teeth at someone, but Priss cannot quite
Make out who when there is still something in her eye. The muscle of

    Bivalves' shells is so extraordinarily strong
It is called a catch. It is extraordinarily difficult to
    Pry it open, to slide the shucking knife into
Its tight mouth. Her father has extraordinary skill. At the mouth
    Of the Rappahannock he holds Virginia in his arms,
Shucking knife at his feet, holding her together, preparing
    Like Priss preparing for yet another Virginia, supposing,
As we all do, that this casual meeting is unsullied by others,
    That there will be only the protecting translucent sheet
Through which she will see as sharply as the meticulous oyster knife
    Slices the muscle's lock, and will not be left to wonder
Why she loves some stranger to the quick, why she takes her
    To herself and why the translucent sheet turns
Opaque in the middle of a sentence like mica thickly layered:
    Sparkling, attracting, reflecting back Priss in Virginia.

Until the middle of the twentieth century, book bindings were sewn together before the adhesion of an outer skin of leather or cloth. Since that time, more and more have been glued, a process known as "perfect binding."

Grossbard's Encyclopedia of Bookbinding

A PERFECT BINDING

Glued rather than sewn. The book cracks in
Parts, falls—paper Niagaras of disrepair.
Its separations come at the most used junctions:
Honeymoons, circular hives where arguments wax and
Wane, where cross words escalate; mechanical stairs
Where the Savior escapes his relatives and mounts Heaven;
The mare, saddled in the house where the Madam mother
Reigns in salty splendor.

These places, read and reread, cause the book
To open to those crucial pages, those we must
Touch, tongue to sore spot on the gum: how he
Loves her, how she loves him, how, like Mohawks
Come West to salvage what they could, to survive
Slaughter, they must live on reservations.
No matter what the ceremonies, death is no longer
Responsible for parting the sheets.
Falling apart is laid to resin, mucilage,
Thick as sex.

What kind of thread or twine, what consummate
Glue or paste can bind a man who cannot bear
To have the crotch of his book touched?
He isolates each volume, shelves it, then, with

Passionate indecision, books a partner, holding
The body, ruffling the pages lightly to assure
No fingerprint or line of fold. Reading and
Rereading, he is riveted, then riven.
Distraught: those unstitched avowals, that
Perfect binding.

THE ERYTHROPHOBIC MAN

Erythrophobia: fear of turning red in public situations

He has to sit through the meeting listening to that fool, deWitt,
Describe the targets, listening to him pin-point them
As if he were a blind-folded four year old, pin and tail in
Fist, aiming for the donkey's ass. And then deWitt
Describes a plan which is a garbled version of the one
Which he, himself, had plotted out so clearly to B and then to B and C.
He can feel the stammer, which he'd never really had,
Tying his tongue, making it hostage to those who speak
In his place, can feel the flush rising
In his face, printing it.

Red blots out deWitt: floods of
Roses, breeching the banks of the Mississippi,
Red petals rising higher than the houses;
Blood spilling from the tubes and plastic sacs in the lab,
Inundating the wards, the private rooms, the O.R.;
Crimson silk moving off Granny's furniture,
Down carved wood legs, across the Orientals, sliding and wrapping.
And he in his crib, reaching for his brother,
Finding himself alone in the red dark.

B whispers to C; the whisper pushes the erythrophobic man out of
His seat. He stands in his black cord suit and white-on-white shirt
To attack. He sees red and turns it,
Not the shy red of the blushing girl, but the battle red
Of the defending man or the gobbling turkey cock
Whose wattles hang like the labia of old women. Avoiding what
He fears, he has become what he avoids:
They have read you, read you.
They have read you like a book.

THOSE WHO LIVE ALONE

When good news comes, wonder why, though they have been
Waiting and waiting for the kettle to work itself into a fury,
Releasing celebratory plumes of steam into the cool air,
Though they have been watching and watching—and the boil
Is so lancingly slow—why then does the actual moment
Lack all lustre? The mind encompasses the message and signals
This is now a time of happiness. Neurons do their work,
Synapses join or snap to attention, whatever they do, all parts
Of the body acknowledge receipt. There is even
A certain amount of action: calls to those who will be pleased,
From those whose voices are feathery with congratulation.
The kettle whistles on in an explosion of vapours
Which should make the one who lives alone faint with joy.

Instead the air fills with damp, foreshadowing twinges
Of loss and other infirmity so at home it settles down as if
To stay. In pleating litanies of inattention, the lacks
Crease themselves more and more sharply into edges until they form
A paper fan which lies beside the blue cup full of amber tea.
Blue cup on green table with white fan. And the one who lives alone,
Admiring the fan, the style of its making, the knife-edge of
Its folds, the precision of its dilemmas, snaps it open and shut,
Open and shut, looking away from the door, the blue door,
Looking away, no longer willing to invite the actual.

SUPPLANTING THE BELOVED

Every time he jogged by that window, he admired
The *Aeonium*: the architecture of its fleshy greens,
The fluid promise of its soft skin. It stood in
The midst of a dazzle of *Aurorae borealae*,
More truculent than they, but somehow
More alluring.

Each day he looked and looked but longed
For more: to fondle, kiss, bite. He jogged other
Routes trying to tamp his vegetable desires for
The objectively ornamental, but
The circling rosettes of its leaves
Blurred the air, making vision so difficult that
He stumbled over roots in the path or
Fell on asphalt.

He was forced not only to return to it
But to get closer, veering off streets onto
The lawn, risking chiropractic
As he twisted his neck to keep the second floor frame
In sight. It burgeoned
Under his scrutiny as if his gaze were nutrient;
It sent forth buds of gala pink from every green
Interstice. In acute dream he tasted flesh but, running,
Averted his face to blades of grass averring
That stubbly green would turn his thoughts from the cannibal act.
Safely home he rolled peas or corn from Hungry Man
TV Dinners on his tongue as if they
Were buds.

~

He considered ringing the door bell, offering
To buy the plant, but he had never believed in
Slavery, and knew that silver nights and the romance
Of the rose or *Aeonium* thrived on denial.
All he allowed himself was an extra meeting,
Jogging each morning as well as when he left
The hardware store. *It* was so beautiful in
The different lights of morning and sunset, its pinks
Bordered like a marquee with globes of dew
Or reddened into evening flush. He raised the sword
Beneath his plushy sweat suit
In chivalrous salute.

The first weeks the woman with the long blond braids
Blushed under his stares as she misted the *Aurorae borealae*.
She baked bread so the odor would waft out
Over the *Aeonium domesticum*, doubling its promises,
And bound her braids into buns, studded with
Jet beads like raisins. She crisped the organdy curtains
To frame her face in ravishments of lace.
When he disappeared for weeks, she tied
The curtains back with black ribbons. When he returned,
Not only returned but bought a new suit and came twice
A day, she allowed her longing to scour away
Her skin of shyness and decided next sunset,
When the curtains would turn rose, to let down
Her hair.

It fell, a shining curtain, almost to the lintel
Of the first floor window. To climb hair is a slippery
And painful business, demanding belief as well as obsession.
Therefore our desires seldom meet and

Those happy endings cannot become the beginnings which
They always were. She puts down the window;
He jogs past the glass seraglio. The *Aeonium*'s root hairs
Grab the soil like fingers and it puts on
A pink show more compelling than the sunset
Reflected in the panes of
The locked windows.

APARTMENTS ON FIRST AVENUE

*Cemeteries are becoming so crowded in the New York area that a
conglomerate has filed plans to construct a block-square above-ground
facility.*

WNYC News broadcast

Underground space, like water, is running out
So they are building apartment houses for the dead.
That ad: "Keep your loved ones safe from seepage," is
Obsolete; these marble skyscrapers have
No cracks and point in the right direction.
Here, where the municipal station tolls the hour with
"This is New York where more than eight million people
Live and work and enjoy the fruits of democracy,"
The question now becomes where can you afford
To live and where to live and die?

Persephone, her lips stained with pomegranate juice,
Runs in her shift (it is 8 to 4) through the hall.
The seeds from that seedy red globe litter;
They cannot root in marble fields. She plays
Her lyre and the single strand of plaint
Turns polyphonous, echo's counterpoint off
Blue-veined cleavage. Here in the clouds, strains
Of the lyre suffuse the thin air, using it up.
But Zeus, her father, angry at the music of women,
Tells her to go to Hades again even though
The bright stamens of her hair make him want to
Stroke it. She resists his direction. Lightning bolts.
O Lord, the hardness of this place.
She takes the elevator down, abasing herself.

~

O Lord, the hardness of this place:
Galleries fitted to entomb feeling and bodies,
Sky catacombs where love's declensions stiffen into
Fixity. But I play my lyre and it tells the truth.
Gluck's single strand of happiness resounds.
If you, walking ahead, searching for a bridge to
That most circular of Museums, turn and
Look at me too long, we may both become marble—
Statues for our funerary niche—but we must risk it.
Pluto, Zeus, our parents, the archangel Michael,
The mayor: to Hell with them. Or not.
You reach out your hand and turn. Pulses deny marble.
The ignited fires have no lick of burning.
Defying the Storm King Power Co., we walk out into
The light fantastic, trip the sidewalks. Within our
Bodies' compass no need to fight gravity.

III   TRACKING CONNECTIONS

*And in spite of the cosmopolitan views on which he prided him-
self, he thanked heaven he was a New Yorker and about to ally
himself with one of his own kind.*

Edith Wharton

The fire in the ice box took place in the subway.
"Damn the ice man," said the conductor on
The Lexington Local, braking to a halt before flames,
"He forgot to deliver the ice." Smoke climbed
To the gritty heaven of the tunnel and up through
The grates in front of Forty-Five East Eighty-Fifth
Where Dorty Tim Kreigh had just come out.
The theme of the party was gardenias, gold rings and
Red velvet hearts in ice cupids, a debutante Valentine's Day.

Leonard stood so long looking at Dorty's eighth floor window
He got a stiff neck—which he kept all his life—
And aroused the suspicions of the doorman at Forty-Five.
She had packed her elopement bag and tried
To climb down the pole of smoke into the arms of
Her dearly beloved and his waiting Stutz Bearcat,
Taking only her tiny bag and her silver fox cape,
But she had to use their back-up plan,
The servant's exit and the downtown platform at Lexington and 86th.

*. . . a city that, like Heaven to them, had existed by faith alone.
All the days of their lives they had heard of it, and it seemed to
them the center of all the glory, all the wealth and all the freedom
in the world. New York. It had an alluring sound.*

Paul Laurence Dunbar

New York adopts the nation's freaks and crazies
Like the Catholic Charities responding to newborns
In garbage pails left at the font. Shorty Gentry,
The dwarf from South Carolina, stood on the Star of David
Made by the rail's intersection and the conductor yelled so,
His saliva arced third rail current, increasing an already
Inflammatory situation. But Shorty stayed calm, picked up
The tongs left by the iceman, and opened the fiery door.
"Melons on fire," he announced and sent those cantaloupes
With their flaming aura spinning down the track
With a whack of his amazingly large right palm,
A favorite of Mme. Shiva Vermont—Reader—and they hit
The blocks of ice the iceman delivered but forgot to put in the box.

> *How this miracle of fire and ice was to be created and to sustain*
> *itself in a harsh world, he had never taken the time to find out.*
> *Edith Wharton*

In New York, present is still past:
Water rises in the cars from the melting ice
And smoke, colored by its source, hangs,
A cantaloupe-grey curtain. Passengers, wet to their ankles,
Certain they will catch cold, choke, sit—no way to get off in
The tunnel—read the *Mirror*, *Tribune*, *Graphic*, *Telegram* and *Eagle*.
Man-made disasters are the daily course;
None natural; hurricanes and locust plagues are stuffed
In concrete envelopes before they touch New Yorkers.

Shorty Gentry enters and offers to lead them out,
But the pomaded Italian turns to the colored woman in
Lime and fuchsia who is reading Dunbar's *The Uncalled*
And they agree to decline because they are so much taller than he
And are unsure of his lineage. The woman in silver fox

Goes into labor; her waters break.
She moans on the woven straw seat.
The conductor turns away; people in charge never are
Though they send their bills anyway.
Shorty says he will deliver her. A vein
In the fontanelle beats a pavane while
The baby, blue as ice or blood, emerges.
Shorty whacks it with his amazingly large palm.
They name her Aurora because of
The melon's sunrise light. It is Groundhog Day, 1928.

> *As* The New York Times *said: /The elevator always seeks out/ the floor of the fire/ and automatically opens and won't shut./ These are warnings/ that you must forget/ if you're climbing out of yourself./ If you're going to smash into the sky.*
>
> *Anne Sexton*

If you are born in New York City, where past is also future,
You will know smoky suffocations and all forms
Of fiery desire. You may confuse course with
Class and never see what is happening above ground.
But Aurora did. She climbed stairs for Shorty's funeral.
And, in spite of pulls toward the old, familiar
IRT, she stayed where she will not know if the stars
Are street lights reflecting in plate glass
Or an Edison map of the subway system or sparks
From the third rail flying through a grating,
Through the air, through the window to sprinkle
The black worsted draping the table where Mme. Shiva Vermont
Slits the seams of the cantaloupe moon.

IN SUCH AN UNHAPPY NEIGHBORHOOD, CARLOS

for Nancy Eimers

The nylon crescent of her pink panties hangs in the sky
And I can't slip on anything or into
Something comfortable because Mama always told me
"You're the man now, now he's gone. Be a good boy,"
But I wouldn't turn down a green silk robe or a bed
Because Mama, listen to me, you know I do wear the pants.

The others were jealous because I was born under
A special moon with the great scorpion rising
And ram horns battering the smeary streak
Of milk in black sky like a needle in
A Carmen Dios record and today I wore grey ones over khakis
Over my jeans because it is cold for July.

And they were jealous because I went to school
And got a round, gold medal and because I knew so much
That they sliced the watermelon into halves like a moon
With that green rim giving warning and they seeded
The dark pink flesh with something because they were jealous
And they wanted me stupid the way they were.

And I bit into the flesh of the melon moon
And Perdita danced for me in her shiny yellow skirt
And I knew I was slipping down Truxillo Street
As if it were a banana peel and broke every bone in my body.
But they didn't get me stupid. All I can see
Is the nylon crescent of her pink panties hanging
On the post on my bed and I keep asking—can't you hear—
When can I see my Mama?

WEDDING BANS: JANUARY 1980

Jack is polishing his black T-bird, new and shiny as a bullet.
I drive by in a cart, which suits me
To a T in chain mail, that silver second skin. The cart, pulled
By a bullock, draws me
To the well where pales of water
Bleach the landscape to the blacks and greys
Of a Chinese scroll—my cart is my heart—my suit.
Poker-playing suitors choose strip, then
Fence, their fire tools crossed swords like those of
Men in Love, or claim they're mine and tear
Trees off hills like bandages to get at seams: the goal,
Coal. My bullock, part of
The scroll scene but not heard, has dull grey hide and silent horns.
Jack flashes by in his bullet Bird, honking,
Driving circles around me. I sip Chinese tea from the à la carte menu
And ignore him.
Tired, he deflates—a nail or tack on the street—and lifts
The black Bird on his back
To change the flat; he is the one and
Only Jack.
His apartment is spare, a good place to store his clubs,
Though the rent is high.

In the seventies we were both right, not politically,
There we were both left, though he stated
I left him and I stated he left me: misstatements
Like unbalanced checkbooks or Byelorussia.
Divorce was necessary-checkmate—
And that is almost always more bitter than
Horseradish or green tea, and it was. Jack took up

Golf, of course, and made a hole in one
Like a burning cigarette on a carpet. I joined a T-group
And removed the ring from my bullock's
Nostrils which, heaven knows, I should have done years ago.
Jack and I were both right. Now we both
Do. The oddsmaker, Jimmy the Greek, says even if our books
Are accepted, only one will win
The Nobel and peel fame like a Mandarin orange.

Campaigning, I use chain mail: "Nominate me and I will
Send you a scrap of silver veil from the days
When I was a nun." Jack, male already, puts chains on the Bird
To get set for the snowy roads of Norway.
When the winner's name is announced, the public, noticing the work,
Cries: author, author. Jack cries fraud.
I cry tears. But you, Will, long awaited, long overdue
Don't duck. You let me tear at you, smooth
My cross feathers until we nest softly down. I spin yarns,
Card wool and promise myself I will never this time
Pull it over your eyes, never even to prevent the intolerable.

The house that Jack built is gone—only the deck remains;
Something always does. With you, new stories rise.
Our building. A spire. And we do. Gold rings
Concentric as sex from the bell. I tell you this,
Will: I love you. Let the bells in the spire peal that.
And if, even in this first month of the decade, that wraps us
In too many rainbows and makes the violins
Lose their fine tune in the romantic damp, we will sing
A cappella. Thank God, we are not alike as
Two peas in a pod. But I warn you without two, capella
Means old she-goat. Or this, you say. Or that, I answer.
In the morning the unaccompanied air will catch,

A mote in the eye or a motet, to vex or delight.
Enough of rowing, let's stow our oars for awhile.

The bed, the boat floats down the brook, *der Bach*,
As tongues of bells and our mouths lick the half-spent night.

This is the day of the night it began to turn,
Like milk, slightly sour, still
So close to freshness one is not sure if
The tongue or the cream is at fault.

He, floundering back toward the bay
Like a suddenly beached fish, cannot see that
The water has changed, as if the dairy plant
Behind him had confused its flows, releasing
All its curds the way defective plants can.

He, lunging toward water, does not know,
Has never had to, that even with the ocean's
Grand dilution the balance of fluids has been
Slightly altered, like the shift of residue in
The ear's circular canals. I, experienced
In acute pain, too full of acuity, know
But do not know why milk
Spoils when it seems fresh.

"Your family has had bad luck," he said last night
Just before he found the clocks had stopped
And indicted the house again. Perhaps that is it.
The stroke of his hand makes time seamless but
The clock strikes, even if unheard, and blood poisoning
(Which killed my father's mother when she used
A knitting needle on the fetus, which killed
My uncle when, even with an open cut, he wore
Blue socks) moves through me into him as we come together.

~

Louis Pasteur, I beg you, seal us in a bottle,
Let us remain bacilli free, save us from relative
Poisons and deaths, from what may prey on us.

It takes awhile to read the ocean,
To see that the prayer is the agent of
What is prayed against. But we've caught it
Early. Let's stop stamping, like spoiled children,
Trying to seal the bargain. Instead
Let's clap our flippers (how I admire
The silvery gloss of sun on your body), spin
Bottles on our noses, beg for
Kippers, and kiss by the beautiful sea.

> *Bending over him, Turandot flings her last riddle at him. "What is*
> *like ice—yet burns?" Suddenly Prince Calaf jumps to his feet. He is*
> *now sure of victory, "The ice that burns—it is Turandot."*
>
> *Synopsis of Puccini's* TURANDOT

My familiar lover:
All too. We ran away from the burrow of family
To meet at the Continental Divide. Apart,
The pieces had fallen into place; together, they fall apart.
Yet from all that tearing up and down and in and out of
Passion's landscape, finally a sigh escapes its prison of ribs
As the awful snow-capped Rockies are glimpsed, then
Confronted. At the pinnacle there is division, of course:
Water flows in opposite directions, blue arteries,
East and West. And snow replaces green as
Rock's embellishment. We stand on the ridge watching
A single mole, a hairy beauty spot against the white
Below. Here, together, our penny dreadful melodramas—
Gaslight flicker, Noh or Passion play, Peking or
Puccini opera—will be played up and down and out and over.

The worst of what is familiar is less likely to maim
Than the moderately bad of what is not. So we
Make neither up nor out nor over, just make sure to guarantee
The worst as we set out the picnic. For me, because my family
Came from Alsace, Weiss and Campagne; for you, from Gdansk,
Kielbasa. Spreading the cloth, you state this is no picnic
And turn to put on the ritual paint, red silk kimono.
Gilt fan in hand, you exhale the gasping music speech as
I dress in lampblack satin, jet beads, a crow boa

And paste a heart-shaped mole on my left cheek. The play
Begins: you use blocks; I, faints. Nothing
Meets; we slice the sausage into familiar declarations.

In spite of the gloss of the scenery, perhaps because of it
There is something sinister here which even the best paraphrase
Cannot put into words, a certain spitefulness thickens
The exhilarating air. Moles thread the snow,
Suggesting subterranean terrors better left unmolested.
Old enough to know it is impossible to change weather or
Landscape, we look at today's parts and try to change them,
Try to braid the twain. Compromise: Turandot. You, still in
Eastern garb, lie down in the snow to ice for the role,
Impressing a perfect Asian angel. I suit up as Calaf who,
Though he won the Empress, his Turandot, would not claim her till
She loved him, too. We perform in Asian fashion:
Man becomes woman, woman, man though your heavy beard,
My wide hips become neither part. Puccini's music echoes against
Channels of rock, flows with water into clefts.
Only when the sky's scar, a lightning bolt, strikes me as
You raise your hand do I realize I am no Calaf but a common suitor
Who does not wish to die for love and therefore will.
Turandot hits high B-flat conveying the rules and penalties.
After the first act we sit down to recast, struggling
For something easy. Making mountains into molehills is not,
Especially when Wagner shimmers in the distance like
Forest fire without trees. Impossible immolation.

Black-brown fur blinks in the drift. We stop
Counting down and up and in and out to push the snow aside
Revealing the squirming litters, dark, moist, quickly
Increasing. Let's take cover in the pulsing, moving bed.
They weave around us, licking, softly probing, warm nest

Of fur, nothing molten. Music: breath in thin air,
A hum, small scale, piano practice instead of
Pageant. We pull up the blanket of snow and cleave together;
Such familiar comfort, my love, we forget what we know.

HYMN IN A BED OF AMHERST

There is a certain chill so deep inside it will not yield
To layers of down or wires telegraphing warmth through wool—
Another quilt upon the mound—no comforts can amend it.
Passion's enactments—flaring, flaming—trumpet heat and melt
The flesh yet—like a stone-graved alphabet—the granite cold
Is there incised and sharp. Even anger's once sure fire
Burns with ice flamed dry. Long lines—extended like a wartime
Queue for meat—accrue no remedy; extension is
A form of prolongation—the poet's cure—but what will be
Prolonged cannot be willed. Nothing is impossible
To understand: one times nought is nought, which leaves one clear
Of lover's rubble. And warm as love conceived in logic's sphere.
When heat resists all stratagems, escape to greater cold,
The wrap of arctic circuses—go North to vault the Pole.

LETTER TO RICHARD FROM BUDAPEST

for Richard Howard

I so enjoyed yours from Beyoglu,
It was a feast: Thanksgiving.
Scimitars carved chunks of sky into
Nocturne portions for you and S. Dressing
And undressing. "Our trip," although we both have stumbled
Several times. The course has changed, nearer dessert,
But don't you find it *does* get sweeter?
If this were Beyoglu—Turkish delight?

But this is Hungary. Here M. and I live in Buda,
Looking at Pest across the river. Ginsberg
Came through last month and proclaimed himself the former,
But all the poets here agree that, sitting on a chair atop
A table, instructing them on instant meditation, he was
The latter. The Danube's winter corrugations divide the city.
No ice. But grey. The sky since I arrived grey suede,
Lining an expensive hat. Swatches of the past are here
And we are swathed in them and covered by them,
Or it, the hat. We live beneath that dome of velvet skin,
Brim stitched to the ground. But we as outsiders
Can only guess, a phantom pain, how tight the stitches are.
I do know though, the spires of Szent Istvan Bazilika
Or Parliament's sharp spikes do not pierce through to clearer air;
And the notes of the pervasive gypsy music arc up,
Fall back, spent arrows like the large meandering snow flakes
Intricate as the windows of Matyas Church.
Mary said, "Bring back some pictures of churches which show
Turkish influence." But though the sky is pocked with onions,

Which I believe are Byzantine, I find I do not know
The Moorish from the Magyar. I see you sighing at my ignorance,
One eyebrow lifted as if you'd spotted a misspelling.

Subways here were built before the ones in NYC. They move as if
On air, cost one forint (14¢), and the entrances
Are open, no turnstiles. But last night I put a forint in
And bear-trap jaws sprang closed in front of me; so difficult,
A foreigner and dumb, to find out when and why they close or don't.
Red stars on top of all official buildings.
Here they would carve Turkey with a sickle
Though they detest all their successive conquerors,
The Russians and the Austrians, as well as Turks.
Last week we went to Wien to see *Der Rosenkavalier*, the trip
M's birthday present. Coffee in the dining car,
A perfect measure of Hungary's position:
Not thick as Turkish, nor thin and strong as Viennese,
But gritty black as coal that heated the compartments.
We sipped. A soldier, hands on hips—quite near his gun—
Moved through, clearing the car before him as the border neared,
Reminder that this boarding house is state-controlled.
We come and go, we foreigners. But those who pension here
Can only cross this line every three years.
And not unless their red stars wink in even rows
As our gold ones did in grammar school.

Breakfast at the Pension Zipser was mocha and sweet crescent rolls.
Their shape a badge of honor for the bakers of Vienna,
A patent given them by Ferdinand the First, in 1683 because
They heard, through their bake-oven walls, the tapping of
Invading Turks who tried to break the city by tunneling
Through the ramparts. At first it seemed the rats

Were hungrier than usual, but soon the bakers
Knew and rang the bells and saved Vienna.

At night the neon stars hover over all and join
The crosses here in Budapest to form a black sky tic-tac-toe.
Knock, knock.
Who's there?
A game I think they do not play here
Where knocks at doors evoke too much.
Red star at night; sailors' delight.
Coal barges on the Danube. But we are of the land.
Ours. And though we love the fiery Paprikas, the Poets' Park
On Margarethe Island and Bartók at the Opera,
The twilight of home does gleam whatever
The slubs in its fabric. A protester at home
Here sees the flag's white stars and field of blue and
Hums our anthem. Tonight we go to *Traviata* in Hungarian;
They started that in 1906 to protest King Franz Josef's edict:
"The word of command may *not* be given in Hungarian." Not only
Did the operas switch, but no recruits enlisted that whole year.

The layers here are not like Dobosh torte, each visible,
More like the Danube on a quiet day:
Each transparent, together opaque as oil.
Red star at night; sailors' delight.
Red star in the morning . . . forgive what may be jingoism.

Love flourishes amidst the fiddlers and the cembalos and,
Yes, amidst the stars. I hope it does for you as well, dear
Richard. Red stars in the grey sky. A galaxy parading.
I will be home in March.

POSTCARD OF CHILD PEEKING OUT FROM
UNDER ITS MOTHER'S SKIRT

for Josef Jarab, the Czech translator

Holding on and letting go: you said that, but
How did you know? Because you are not the artist,
Perspective protectively out of kilter, whose
Sideways glance at the work dances off it
Like angled sun on a glass window.

What does a bagpiper wear under his kilt?
He puffs into the sheep bladder and under there
The effort of air inflates his scrotum. He rides a balloon,
Thinking it is the ecstasy of music, of
"The Dirge for Scottish Lassies," and is sure his kilt
Conceals more than the question of underwear.

    Knock, knock.
    Who's there? Kilt.
    Kilt who? Cock Robin.
    Holding on and the ultimate letting go.

What does Confucius hide under his silken robe? He sits
In the Palace of Celestial Jade and with
A fluent twist of wrist brushes onto paper:
    All writing is translation as
    The moon translates the sun.

He dips into a blue china cup
Full of black ink, and wields his brush with death,
Avoiding it by what he passes on.

Stirring between his legs, is his son.
See him peeking out from under Father's skirts.

    Knock, knock.
    Who's there? Man.
    Man who? Man Peking out of child.

The poet skirts the issue: a boy and a girl,
Holding on and letting go, life and death.
Josef, you will understand these are for you:
A photo of a woman in her skirt of many shades.
Love. Books written and read. We will join what we can
And where, adjusting glosses in our alchemical tinkering.

KNOCK, KNOCK

He pulls open the door, newly painted, and
Walks into the wall on which it was propped.
The door drops forward, hitting him on the head,
Knocking the TV from its stand to the floor
Where the picture tube shatters, exploding
Casablanca—the myth of love forever—into
His left hand, right leg and the back of
The sleeping dog. Wounded by glass,
Head lumped by the unattached, he bounces back to
Pontificate, Sidney Greenstreet or Charlie Chaplin,
Bulge of comic props stretched thin as menace.

And she? His key no longer fits her bonny
And a wall is impressed on his face so
It is time to escape. She runs. Runs from
His imposition. Down stairs. She is fleet.
A token. The train. Coney Island.
The closed amusement park. Alone. But he
May be close behind; he often is. She hides
In the Casbah Tunnel of Love and sure enough
There is a knock on prop wood,
The pink and green ply of false Mosque:
"Who's there?"
"My."
"My who?"
"My new bonny lies over the ocean. But
Come out. I need you."

She'd known and knew, women do, that
When a man pulls open an unattached door

He is announcing his new true love and will
Murder the old if he can; what is unbearable
Should not have to be borne. He pulls open
The false door and walks into another wall.
Knock out. Chance for a getaway. She swims
The tunnel's dirty streams till one leads
To Sheepshead Bay. It lies under the moon,
Black and silver as a hound. Or a cover.
She slips in, pulling the sheet of water over
Her body. Letting go. Holding on to the salty hem,
She sleeps by the beautiful sea.

THE RIVER HONEY QUEEN BESS

I

In May it drops down fresh from the mountains,
Dashing silver flakes of water like mica in the air.
Such abundance foils the stones' and hearts' resistance.
    The five dare not broach their wish to dance with water.
    This is the season of their odes.

Early July and not much rain. The pulse slows. Rocks still
Force froth, but the rush is spent. Puckering white
At the selvedge, its weave of blue and green unfurls.
    Three men, two women are rapt in it.
    This is the season of their proposals.

August, and what has always been at the bottom is seen:
Tires, shoes, water moccasins, coral snakes
Braiding in the mud; and what is culturing in
The mirror plates now glazed false blue?
    "A pox on rivers; we always knew," they say.
    This is the season of their attempted escapes.

After the swellings and fevers abate,
The suitors drape themselves in velvet blue and green
To conceal August scars, and order spring-bottled water,
Hoping glass will contain the uncontrollable.
Before they can begin to drink, a swarm escapes—
Gold-dazzle, noise, honey, sting—a circle
Around each head, a crown of May bees.

Truth has been concealed, like 15th-century meat
Rotting under its fabric of spices. Seasons
Have their progression and this is misleading:
The fool's gold suitors believe if May had lasted
They would have found their beloved. Four leave,
Mourning the march of months, the thwarting procession.
But Will stays, through winter's seeming stasis
When blood becomes manageable, to have the Honey Queen again.

This year, no one knows why—a record snowfall? the drift of
Lava ash over the sun? fatigue, sheer as
The cliff beside the river?—June does not begin
On its appointed date. He has not only the month
But its extension to try to pull the river's winding sheet
Through his gold ring, the wedding band which
Plays *The Water Music*. But though he cannot handle
The river which refuses to be treated like
A scarf, he finds he knows her.

August discoveries are not the fault of August. Under
The river's cloak, under the course of its blue blood
Is a slut, a gutter of water and men. The thirst of love
Is slaked by cloacal knowledge. What should Will do?
Cross himself or the river? What can he afford?

He goes to Raleigh to buy the river valley, to build
The Mother Goose Enchanted Village. No more brooding.
Between "The Queen Is in the Parlour Eating Bread and
Honey Golden Manse" and "The Jack Fell Down
and Broke His Crown Hill," the water wends. Will has it
Paved with silver glass, assuring safe reflection; he bends
To face himself. Through flowered banks the mirrored river curves;
Underneath, Honey Queen Bess sings her sting-green music.

SERIAL RESCUE

The cool water of the running stream may be scooped up with open, overflowing palms. It cannot be grasped up to the mouth with clenched fists, no matter what thirst motivates our desperate grab.

Sheldon Kopp, IF YOU MEET THE BUDDHA ON THE ROAD, KILL HIM

The frog squats on the road, radiating wisdom;
His skin shines, reflecting that supreme being, the sun,
His bent legs, eternal green as eternal spring, assure
The capacity to jump obstacles. I beg him
For tales of enlightenment to end my confusion.
He releases tadpoles into the air, vitreous floaters
Which can be seen only by the avoiding eye.

As soon as I begin to believe we are bound for ever after
I take my knife and stab him, but he smiles
His serene Buddha smile and says, "Here is your mantra:
Is the voice of the frog the voice of death?"
Night is coming on, its blue curtain streaked with
The coral of water lilies. He sits on them, pad to pad.
Smears of ink grow to bolts as my despair deepens.

A new plan spawns. I kiss him over and over,
Making imprints on green skin. But he will not change himself
And I am greening here in the country of the Frog Buddha.
My lids thicken. Heavy. As I drowse
I see in the distance the castle of sleepers
And await the rescuer who will rip me from dream.

And, yes, at last he comes. Asleep, I feel
The appointed Prince approach my couch, hear the slight crack of his knees

As he bends to give his eye-opening kiss. I wait
For the veil of air to waver. "What's this?" he says.
"Chamberlain, come here; I cannot . . . will not . . . even for a kingdom."
He turns from my slick, green skin as if I had hopped from
A seepage bog straight into his astonished mouth.

Waking by myself I realize that I have
And turn to meet the frog. We smile as he invites me
To join him for dinner; we discuss restaurants,
Moving at last into the realm of the ordinary.
But there are always the remnant licks of abandoned obsession;
The minute tear in the cornea which admits light as
A kind of color blindness. A green splinter under the fingernail
Of the finger of the hand holding the fork at the comfortable meal.

Because as they cut it was that special green, they decided
To make a woman of the fresh hay. They wished to lie in green, to wrap
Themselves in it, light but not pale, silvered but not grey.
Green and ample, big enough so both of them could shelter together
In any of her crevices, the armpit, the join
Of hip and groin. They—who knew what there was to know, about baling
The modern way with hay so you rolled it up like a carpet,
Rather than those loose stacks—they packed the green body tight
So she wouldn't fray. Each day they moulted her to keep her
Green and soft. Only her hair was allowed to ripen into yellow tousle.

The next weeks whenever they stopped cutting they lay with her.
She was always there, waiting, reliable, their green woman.
She gathered them in, yes she did,
Into the folds of herself, like the mother they hadn't had.
Like the women they had had, only more pliant, more graceful,
Welcoming in a way you never just found.
They not only had the awe of taking her,
But the awe of having made her. They drank beer
Leaning against the pillow of her belly
And one would tell the other, "Like two Adams creating."
And they marveled as they placed
The cans at her ankles, at her neck, at her wrists so she
Glittered gold and silver. They adorned what they'd made.
After harrowing they'd come to her, drawing
The fountains of the Plains, the long line
Of irrigating spray and moisten her up.
And lean against her tight, green thighs to watch buzzards
Circle black against the pink stain of the sunset.

~

What time she began to smolder they never knew—
Sometime between night when they'd left her
And evening when they returned. Wet, green hay
Can go a long time smoldering before you notice. It has a way
Of catching itself, of asserting that
There is no dominion over it but the air. And it flares suddenly
Like a red head losing her temper, and allows its long bright hair
To tangle in the air, letting you know again
That what shelters you can turn incendiary in a flash.
And then there is only the space of what has been,
An absence in the field, memory in the shape of a woman.

A NOTE ABOUT THE AUTHOR

Cynthia Macdonald was born in New York City, and received her B.A. from Bennington College and her M.A. from Sarah Lawrence College. She has taught at Sarah Lawrence and Johns Hopkins University and is now a professor at the University of Houston, where she founded the creative writing program in 1979. Since 1972, she has published three collections of poems, *Amputations*, *Transplants*, and *(W)holes*. Her grants and awards include a National Endowment for the Arts grant, a Guggenheim Fellowship, and a National Academy and Institute of Arts and Letters Award in recognition of her achievement in poetry. Cynthia Macdonald has also had a career as a singer—singing thirty-five different roles with a number of small opera companies. She is currently in psychoanalytic training at the Houston-Galveston Psychoanalytic Institute.

A NOTE ON THE TYPE

This book was set on the Linotype in Granjon, a type named after Robert Granjon. George W. Jones based his designs for this type upon that used by Claude Garamond (c. 1480–1561) in his beautiful French books. Granjon more closely resembles Garamond's own type than do the various modern types that bear his name. Robert Granjon began his career as type cutter in 1523 and was one of the first to practice the trade of type founder apart from that of printer.

Composed, printed, and bound by
Heritage Printers, Inc., Charlotte, North Carolina

Typography and binding design
by Dorothy Schmiderer